24 HOUR HISTORY

THE ASSASSINATION OF MARTIN LUTHER KING JR

4 APRIL 1968

D1419806

Terry Collins

raintree
a Capstone company — publishers for children

Raintree is an imprint of Capstone Global Library
Limited, a company incorporated in England and Wales
having its registered office at 7 Pilgrim Street, London,
EC4V 6LB – Registered company number: 6695582

www.raintreepublishers.co.uk
myorders@raintreepublishers.co.uk

Text © Capstone Global Library Limited 2014
First published in hardback in 2014
Paperback edition first published in 2015
The moral rights of the proprietor have been asserted.

Edited by Adam Miller, Abby Colich, and
    John-Paul Wilkins
Designed by Steve Mead
Original illustrations © Advocate Art 2014
Illustrated by Dante Ginevra
Production by Victoria Fitzgerald
Originated by Capstone Global Library Ltd
Printed and bound in China

ISBN 978 1 406 27366 3
17 16 15 14 13
10 9 8 7 6 5 4 3 2 1

ISBN 978 1 406 27372 4
18 17 16 15
10 9 8 7 6 5 4 3 2 1

A full catalogue record for this book is available from
the British Library.

Acknowledgements
We would like to tha...
...her invaluable help...

Every effort has bee...
of material reprodu...
be rectified in subse...
the publisher.

All the internet add...
were valid at the tim...
the dynamic nature...
have changed, or si...
exist since publicati...
regret any inconvenience this may cause readers, no
responsibility for any such changes can be accepted by
either the author or the publisher.

CONTENTS

Direct quotations are indicated by a yellow background.

Direct quotations appear on the following pages: 5, 6, 7, 8, 9.

Montgomery, Alabama, USA, 5 December 1955

We are all in agreement of the wrongs done to our dear sister...

Dr Martin Luther King Jr agrees to become the president of the Montgomery Improvement Association (MIA).

The association organizes a boycott of all Montgomery buses by the black community to protest what had happened to Rosa Parks four days earlier.

We also know things will not change overnight, or in a day, or a week, or a month.

Patience, friends. Patience is our ally here.

Parks was arrested after breaking segregation laws by refusing to give up her seat to a white man.

The speech is a passionate cry for justice during the civil rights movement's March on Washington for Jobs and Freedom.

A PRIZE FOR PEACE

On 10 December 1964, Dr King receives the Nobel Peace Prize in Oslo, Norway. The award recognizes his efforts to use non-violent means to end segregation and racial discrimination. Gunnar Jahn, Chairman of the Nobel Committee, notes:

"Today we pay tribute to Martin Luther King, the man who has never abandoned his faith in the unarmed struggle he is waging, who has suffered for his faith, who has been imprisoned on many occasions, whose home has been subject to bomb attacks, whose life and the lives of his family have been threatened, and who nevertheless has never faltered."

STRIKE!

On 12 February 1968, over 1,000 black sanitation workers went on strike in the city of Memphis, Tennessee. The men took a stand for better working conditions. They protested low wages, few or no benefits, and racial slurs from white supervisors. When the city refused to negotiate, Dr King was asked to lend his support.

On 18 March, King made a personal appearance and spoke in Memphis. He returned on 28 March to lead a march down Beale Street for the striking workers. To his horror, violence erupted. Windows were broken and shops were looted. When police arrived, marchers threw stones. Authorities responded with tear gas. At least one marcher was shot.

King was deeply troubled by these events during a march under his leadership. He quickly scheduled another march on 8 April. However, the city of Memphis used the power of the federal government to refuse King permission to stage his demonstration. Ironically, the main reason for this federal injunction was fear for King's safety.

*Andrew Young: Young was a close friend of King and a fellow member of the SCLC. He attended the court hearing with King's lawyer, Chauncey Eskridge.

Ray is ready for the next step of his plan.

Now, all he needs to do is wait for Dr King to reveal himself.

*Chitlins are pigs' intestines that have been cooked as food. They are a popular dish in the American South.

As good as the view from his room is, using a weapon there is not possible. To get a line of sight to shoot at King, Ray needs a better angle.

Such an angle is available from the window of the communal bathroom at the end of the hall.

The Remington Gamemaster is a powerful weapon; overkill, really, for the task at hand.

What thoughts go through the head of an assassin as he tracks his prey?

What is Ray thinking as he loads his rifle with soft-pointed bullets, designed to cause maximum damage to a victim?

The dark corridors of Ray's mind remain private.

A single bullet is all that is required to topple a leader of men.

A single bullet.

Hey! Did you hear that noise?

6:15 P.M.

St Joseph Hospital. Despite the heroic efforts of the doctors, King's injuries are too serious for him to be saved.

7:05 P.M.

Dr Martin Luther King Jr never regains consciousness. He dies that night at 7.05 p.m. But his legacy lives on.

CONCLUSION: THE DREAM ENDURES

Dr Martin Luther King Jr died on 4 April 1968, at the tragically young age of 39. The civil rights movement lost not only a leader, but also the voice of a generation. However, King's work continued after his passing, with his friends and followers taking up the torch for equal rights for all citizens. His close friend, Ralph Abernathy, stepped into King's role as the president of the Southern Christian Leadership Conference (SCLC). He led a peaceful demonstration down the streets of Memphis on 8 April as planned. A pall of mourning hung over the marchers, but so did a sense of determination that King's work was not finished and would not die with him.

President Lyndon B. Johnson said upon learning of King's assassination: "We can achieve nothing by lawlessness and divisiveness among the American people. It is only by joining together and only by working together that we can continue to move toward equality and fulfillment for all of our people." Johnson was a longtime supporter of civil rights and signed the Civil Rights Act of 1964, which prohibited discrimination of all kinds based on race, colour, religion, or national origin. He knew that once grieving for the fallen leader was over, two things would occur. One of them would be the continuing progress of the civil rights movement. The other would be a thirst for justice in the capture of King's killer.

A degree of closure would come with the capture and conviction of James Earl Ray, the shooter who robbed the world of King's presence. An escaped convict with a series of previous stays in prison, Ray remained at large for months. As investigators pieced together the evidence Ray left behind, they knew who their assassin was. The only thing left was to find Ray and let him stand trial.

Ray was arrested, tried, and sentenced for his crime. Dr Martin Luther King's murderer would spend the rest of his life in prison, watching as King's legacy lived on. He died in prison on 23 April 1998.

Just days after King's death, President Johnson signed the Civil Rights Act of 1968, prohibiting discrimination in the sale, rent, and financing of housing. The Act further demonstrated Johnson's commitment to civil rights, and his determination to achieve something significant on behalf of King's legacy. In 1971, the Supreme Court upheld busing as a legitimate way to achieve integration of public schools. As recently as 1991, another Civil Rights Act was signed by then president George H. W. Bush to strengthen civil rights laws and provide for damages in cases of intentional employment discrimination.

Dr Martin Luther King Jr's legacy still lives on today.

TIMELINE

1 February 1968	Memphis, Tennessee, USA. Sanitation workers Robert Walker and Echol Cole are both killed in a horrific dustbin lorry accident when the rubbish compactor malfunctions.
12 February 1968	Over 1,000 black employees from the Memphis Public Works department go on strike due to substandard working conditions, including safety issues
18 March 1968	King speaks to a crowd of over 15,000 supporters of the strike in Memphis, and agrees to lead a protest march
28 March 1968	The march erupts in violence, shocking King and drawing strong criticism of the striking workers. King vows to return to Memphis for a second protest march.

3 April 1968

10.55 a.m.	King and his staff arrive by aeroplane in Memphis and check into the Lorraine Motel
1.00 p.m.	Word of a federal injunction against any demonstration led by King is received. The court says there will be no march.
9.00 p.m.	King makes an impassioned speech at the Mason Temple and renews his pledge to lead a second march

4 April 1968

8.00 a.m. – 4.00 p.m.	King spends the day at the Lorraine Motel, holding meetings and waiting for word from the court about the injunction
3.25 p.m.	James Earl Ray books into a room at Bessie Brewer's boarding house
4.06 p.m.	Ray purchases a set of binoculars to monitor King at the Lorraine Motel
5.00 p.m.	King receives good news. The US District Court has agreed to allow a tightly controlled march on 8 April.

The times given in this book are approximate and may vary between sources.

5.10 p.m.	James Earl Ray starts his surveillance of the door of King's room through his binoculars, waiting for his target to emerge
5.55 p.m.	Gathering with a group of his staff, King prepares to leave the Lorraine Motel for a dinner at the home of a local minister. He stops on the balcony outside his room to talk to his driver, who is waiting down below.
6.01 p.m.	Ray takes aim and fires a single shot, striking King in the upper jaw and damaging his jugular vein and windpipe. The bullet travels downward, cutting King's spinal cord.
6.02 p.m.	Fleeing the boarding house, Ray leaves the murder weapon behind in a doorway on the street before leaving the scene in a white Ford Mustang
6.09 p.m.	The mortally wounded King is carried by ambulance to St Joseph Hospital
7.05 p.m.	Dr Martin Luther King Jr is pronounced dead at St Joseph Hospital
5 April 1968	President Lyndon B. Johnson declares 7 April as a national day of mourning
8 April 1968	The planned march through Memphis goes on as scheduled, now in memorial of the slain King
9 April 1968	More than 50,000 people accompany King's coffin through Atlanta, Georgia, to its final resting place at South View Cemetery
8 June 1968	Ray, under a variety of aliases, has remained at large, but is finally arrested in London, England, at Heathrow Airport
19 July 1968	An extradited James Earl Ray arrives in Memphis to stand trial for the assassination of Dr King
10 March 1969	Ray pleads guilty to killing King, and receives a life sentence of 99 years in Brushy Mountain State Penitentiary in Tennessee
23 April 1998	James Earl Ray dies in prison at the age of 70

CAST OF CHARACTERS

Ralph Abernathy (1926–1990)

King's best friend and second in command of the Southern Christian Leadership Conference (SCLC), Abernathy was born in Linden, Alabama, on 11 March 1926. A World War II veteran, Abernathy graduated from Alabama State University with a degree in mathematics in 1950 and an MA in sociology from Atlanta University in 1951. He became the pastor of the First Baptist Church in Montgomery, Alabama, where he first met King. After King's tragic shooting, Abernathy accompanied his friend in the ambulance to St Joseph Hospital. He succeeded him as SCLC president and continued King's philosophy of using non-violent resistance to achieve equality for African Americans. Abernathy died in Atlanta on 17 April 1990.

Jesse Jackson (b. 1941)

Born on 8 October 1941 in Greenville, South Carolina, Jackson was a member of King's staff and witnessed the shooting of his friend and leader at the Lorraine Motel. A powerful speaker and Baptist preacher, Jackson has never stopped working for the rights of minorities. He campaigned as a Democratic presidential nominee in both the 1984 and 1988 elections, and went on to assist in the release of several US hostages held internationally. In 1989, Jackson received the Spingarn Medal from the National Association for the Advancement of Colored People (NAACP) for outstanding achievement by an African American. The award was presented for Jackson's lifetime achievements in civil rights.

Dr Martin Luther King Jr (1929–1968)

King was born in Atlanta, Georgia, on 15 January 1929. Both his father and grandfather were Baptist preachers, and Martin followed in the family tradition. He attended Morehouse College and Crozer Theological Seminary and received his doctorate of theology from Boston University. King was later influenced by the peaceful teachings of Gandhi and the philosophy of civil disobedience through non-violent protest. Thanks to his powerful intellect and charismatic speaking skills, he became the unofficial leader of the civil rights movement. His words and passion led to the March on Washington to highlight the need for civil rights. On 28 August 1963, over 200,000 people gathered at the Lincoln Memorial to hear King's "I Have a Dream" speech. He was awarded the Nobel Peace Prize in 1964.

James Earl Ray (1928–1998)

One of eight children, Ray was a mediocre student and failed member of the US Army before he turned to crime. Born on 10 March 1928, in Alton, Illinois, his family was extremely poor. After leaving the armed forces, Ray worked several dead-end jobs before moving to Los Angeles, California, in 1949, where he was promptly arrested for burglary. A series of arrests for fraud and armed robbery followed throughout the 1950s, until he was sentenced to 20 years for armed robbery in 1959. Ray escaped in 1967 and travelled throughout North America under a series of aliases until he assassinated Dr Martin Luther King Jr. Ray's reasons for the murder remain unclear, other than racial hatred and possible recognition for such a high-profile killing. Sentenced to 99 years, Ray died in prison on 23 April 1998, aged 70.

Andrew Young (b. 1932)

The accomplishments of Andrew Young are many. Born on 12 March 1932 in New Orleans, Louisiana, Young went on to serve as one of King's chief aides and the executive director of the SCLC from 1964 to 1970. A graduate of Howard University and Hartford Theological Seminary, he was ordained a minister in 1955. After his time with the SCLC, he represented the state of Georgia in the US House of Representatives in 1972, leaving only to become the US Ambassador to the United Nations in 1978. After resigning from this post in 1979, Young was elected Mayor of Atlanta, Georgia, in 1981, where he served for two successful terms. He continues to write and speak about world politics and civil rights.

GLOSSARY

aide person who gives support on something

alias made-up name

association group of people who have joined together for a common cause

communal belonging to members of a community

cosmic relating to the universe

creed set of beliefs held by a person or group

discrimination unfair treatment of people because of their skin colour, sex, or personal beliefs

equality condition of being equal

extradite transfer a person accused of a crime from one state or country to the country in which the crime was committed

falter become unsure or unsteady; hesitate

infrared form of technology that uses invisible bands of radiation, enabling the user to see in the dark

injunction order from a court to stop someone from doing something

musing deep thought or reflection on something

patience ability to stay calm and wait

perception ability to see, hear, or become aware of something through the senses

quarry living creature that is being hunted

segregation practice of separating people into groups, especially by race

slur negative remark

FIND OUT MORE

Books

Child of the Civil Rights Movement, Paula Young Shelton and Raul Colon (Schwartz & Wade, 2013)

I Have a Dream..., Levi David Addai (Collins Educational, 2013)

*I Have a Dream: Martin Luther King and the Fight for Equal Right*s (One Shot), Anita Ganeri (Franklin Watts, 2013)

Martin Luther King Jr., Michael Teitelbaum (Campfire Graphic Novels, 2013)

DVDs

Dr. Martin Luther King Jr.: A Historical Perspective (Delta Home Entertainment, 2005)

Face to Face (2entertain, 2009)

King: Man of Peace in a Time of War (Passport International, 2007)

The Rosa Parks Story (Xenon, 2003)

Websites

www.archives.gov/research/jfk/select-committee-report/part-2a.html
A report of the Select Committee on Assassinations of the US House of Representatives regarding the King Assassination. Its findings, interviews, and collected evidence concur that James Earl Ray fired a single shot and killed Dr King.

crdl.usg.edu/events/mlk_assassination
A page with letters, legal documents, photographs, sound recordings, FBI files, oral histories, and historical news clips about the assassination and the aftermath.

www.history.com/topics/martin-luther-king-assassination
This collection covering King's assassination features a photo gallery, video clips, an interactive timeline, and much more.

www.thekingcenter.org
The King Center features an extensive online collection of the works and papers of Dr King. The website was introduced in 2011, and the goal is to eventually digitize more than one million documents, with new content being added regularly from the King Center Archive collection.

Places to visit

If you are ever in the United States, you could visit one of these historic sites, which provide a wealth of information about the life and death of Martin Luther King Jr.

Martin Luther King, Jr. National Historic Site
450 Auburn Avenue, NE
Atlanta, GA 30312-1525
www.nps.gov/malu

Martin Luther King, Jr. National Memorial
900 Ohio Drive SW
Washington DC 20024
www.nps.gov/mlkm/index.htm

National Civil Rights Museum at the Lorraine Motel
450 Mulberry Street
Memphis, TN 38103
www.civilrightsmuseum.org

INDEX